NOTE TO PARENTS

Welcome to Kingfisher Readers! This program is designed to help young readers build skills, confidence, and a love of reading as they explore their favorite topics.

These tips can help you get more from the experience of reading books together. But remember, the most important thing is to make reading fun!

Tips to Warm Up Before Reading

- Look through the book with your child. Ask them what they notice about the pictures.
- Wonder aloud together. Ask questions and make predictions. What will this book be about? What are some words we could expect to find on these pages?

While Reading

- Take turns or read together until your child takes over.
- Point to the words as you say them.
- When your child gets stuck on a word, ask if the picture could help. Then think about the first letter too.
- Accept and praise your child's contributions.

After Reading

- Look back at the things your child found interesting. Encourage connections to other things you both know.
- Draw pictures or make models to explore these ideas.
- Read the book again soon, to build fluency.

With five distinct levels and a wealth of appealing topics, the Kingfisher Readers series provides children with an exciting way to learn to read about the world around them. Enjoy!

Ellie Costa, M.S. Ed.
Literacy Specialist, Bank Street School for Children, New York

KINGFISHER READERS

level 2

In the Rainforest

WITHDRAWN

Claire Llewellyn and
Thea Feldman

KINGFISHER
NEW YORK

KINGFISHER
LONDON & NEW YORK

Copyright © Kingfisher 2014
Published in the United States by Kingfisher,
175 Fifth Ave., New York, NY 10010
Kingfisher is an imprint of Macmillan Children's Books, London.
All rights reserved.

Distributed in the U.S. and Canada by Macmillan,
175 Fifth Ave., New York, NY 10010

Library of Congress Cataloging-in-Publication data has been applied for.

Series editor: Thea Feldman
Literacy consultant: Ellie Costa, Bank Street College, New York

ISBN: 978-0-7534-7144-9 (HB)
ISBN: 978-0-7534-7145-6 (PB)

Kingfisher books are available for special promotions and
premiums. For details contact: Special Markets Department,
Macmillan, 175 Fifth Ave., New York, NY 10010.

For more information, please visit
www.kingfisherbooks.com

Printed in China
9 8 7 6 5 4 3 2 1
1TR/0913/WKT/UG/105MA

Contents

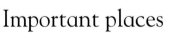

A hot, rainy place

A rainforest is a forest where it rains a lot, and temperatures are about 80°F (27°C).

Rainforests are found
near the **equator**.

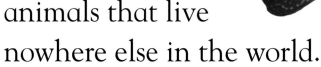

They each have
many plants and
animals that live
nowhere else in the world.

Rainforest plants

Plants grow well in a warm,
wet, and sunny place.

They grow all year long
in a rainforest.

Trees are
the world's
tallest plants.

Some trees in
rainforests
can be 200 feet
(61 meters) tall.

Plants provide food

Rainforest plants provide food
for many animals.

The animals eat the stems, leaves,
flowers, and fruit of the plants.

Animals also find shelter
in rainforest plants.

Life at every layer

Trees and other plants grow at their own special height in a rainforest. This is called a layer.

Animals are at every level or layer.

Some live high up in the **canopy**.

Big animals, like the jaguar, live on the ground.

Some plant eaters

Leaf-cutter ants live in rainforests in South America.

They chop leaves with their strong jaws.

Hummingbirds eat
nectar from flowers
in a rainforest canopy.

Monkeys eat fruit
that grows on
tree branches.

Some meat eaters

Some animals in a rainforest
eat other animals.

They are called meat eaters
or predators.

Eagles in the canopy
catch monkeys or **sloths**
in their sharp claws.

Tarantulas on the ground
grab insects, frogs, or mice
with their long fangs.

Speaking up

Rainforests are so leafy that
it can be hard for some animals
to see each other.

So they make noise!
Frogs croak, birds squawk,
and monkeys howl.

Animals also call out to warn
each other about dangers.

Bright colors

Some animals have bright colors that are easy to see in a green forest.

Birds like these can find mates because of their bright colors.

Brightly colored rainforest frogs
have dangerous **poisons** in them.

Their colors warn predators
not to eat them.

Blending in

Some animals are hard to find because their colors or shapes help them blend into the forest.

This stick insect and lizard use **camouflage** to hide from predators.

Some predators, like the ocelot,
blend into the forest too,
so they can sneak up on their **prey**.

Rainforest rivers

Rain puts even more water into rainforest streams and rivers.

Many animals live in rainforest rivers.

Long snakes called anacondas,
small alligators called caimans,
and fish with sharp teeth
called piranhas all live in
rainforest rivers in South America.

Village life

People have lived in rainforests for
thousands of years.

Today they live in villages,
in houses made of wood and leaves.

They know which plants are good to eat, and which can be used to help heal sicknesses.

They know how to hunt and fish too.

Vanishing places

Rainforests around the world are being destroyed.

Trees are being chopped down and sold as lumber.

The land is also being cleared
so roads and farms can be built.

In some cleared rainforests,
people dig **mines** in the ground.

Important places

Rainforests are important for
our planet.

They provide places for thousands
of plants and animals to live.

Many of the plants are sources
of food for people too.

Trees also send **oxygen** into
the air, which we all need
to breathe.

Saving rainforests

Now there are reserves
in some rainforests.

Reserves are places where
plants and animals
are protected.

Many people are working
to save the rainforests
of the world.

Our planet
would not
be the same
without these
special places!

Glossary

canopy one of the highest levels of trees in a rainforest

camouflage (say *CAM-uh-floj*) the color or shape of an animal that helps it blend in with its surroundings

equator an imaginary line around the middle of Earth

mine a deep hole dug into the ground from which people dig out gold, tin, or other things

nectar a sweet liquid found inside flowers

oxygen a gas in the air that all people and animals need to breathe in order to survive.

poison something that can make people and animals sick or kill them if they swallow it

prey an animal that is hunted for food

sloth a slow-moving animal in South America that lives in rainforest trees

If you have enjoyed reading
this book, look out for more in
the Kingfisher Readers series!

Collect
and read
them all!

KINGFISHER READERS: LEVEL 2

Fur and Feathers ☐
In the Rainforest ☐
Trucks ☐
What Animals Eat ☐
Where Animals Live ☐
Where We Live ☐
Your Body ☐

KINGFISHER READERS: LEVEL 3

Ancient Rome ☐
Cars ☐
Creepy-Crawlies ☐
Dinosaur World ☐
Firefighters ☐
Record Breakers—The Biggest ☐
Volcanoes ☐

For a full list of Kingfisher Readers books, plus
guidance for teachers and parents and activities
and fun stuff for kids, go to the Kingfisher Readers
website: **www.kingfisherreaders.com**